M000026189

ex libris

....

PENGUIN BOOKS

Published by the Penguin Group

Penguin Books Ltd, 27 Wrights Lane, London W8 5TZ, England

Penguin Putnam Inc., 375 Hudson Street, New York,
New York 10014, USA

Penguin Books Australia Ltd, Ringwood, Victoria, Australia

Penguin Books Canada Ltd, 10 Alcorn Avenue,
Toronto, Ontario, Canada M4V 3B2

Penguin Books (NZ) Ltd, Private Bag 102902, N5MC,
Auckland, New Zealand

Penguin Books Ltd

Registered Offices: Harmondsworth, Middlesex, England

First published by Penguin Books 1998

1 3 5 7 9 10 8 6 4 2

Copyright this collection © Penguin Books Australia Ltd, 1998

Typeset in Granjon

Printed in England by William Clowes Ltd

ISBN 0–140–27979–2

The Little Book of

GAY
LOVE

For Derek.

Not for Christmas, not for
our birthday but just
because you are gay. With love
Dad and
Mags.

PENGUIN BOOKS

Love has always been the only
thing that is truly radical, because
it releases all prisoners.

Gavin Dillard

Your love was wonderful to me,
passing the love of women.

David to Jonathan (2 Samuel 1:26)

He who desires but acts not,
breeds pestilence.

William Blake

Jane rode around on a Harley-bike
To strangers she looked
just like a bull dyke
But at home in bed,
To her lover she pled:
'Get the ribbons.
You know what I like.'

Anonymous

Is that a gun in your pocket
or is your penis engorged with blood?

Julian Clary

Every straight guy should have a man's tongue in his mouth at least once.

Madonna

Don't be so prissy, darling,
excitement isn't always clean.

John Waters

God didn't create homosexuals so people would have someone to hate.

Reverend Shelagh Zincke

I've never been tempted by God
but I like his trappings.

Jeanette Winterson

You always have to remember – no matter what you're told – that God loves all the flowers, even the wild ones that grow on the side of the highway.

Cyndi Lauper

Before the flowers
of friendship faded
friendship faded.

Gertrude Stein

My joy was unbounded
and I cannot imagine it greater,
even if love had been added.

André Gide

Nothing is so small it can't be
blown out of all proportion.

Rita Mae Brown

Inconvenient as it may be, the reality is that one can have great sex with someone one neither loves nor likes; indeed under the right circumstances hatred is an effective aphrodisiac.

Dennis Altman

Hate is not a family value.

slogan

Simply the thing I am
shall make me live.

Shakespeare

What I'd forgotten was that he was not
Parsifal and I was not the Grail; the
medievalism of my imagination was not
sufficiently up-to-date to recognize that
the lover was a shopper and I a product.

Edmund White

The love of boys is sweet.
Even the king of gods,
the son of Kronos,
loved a boy Ganymede.

Theognis of Megara

The prettier they are, the prettier they want to be – and the less work they want to do in the sack.

Mark Trevorrow

All received information
should make us inverts sad.
But before I finish I intend to celebrate
our corner of Paradise, the part of the
garden the Lord forgot to mention.

Derek Jarman

I have a wild and raucous sex life,
okay? I leave it up to your imagination.

Gregg Araki

The word 'lover' is always more than non-gay people want to know.

Shelly Roberts

I think extreme heterosexuality
is a perversion.

Margaret Mead

We live in the lesbian capital of London, we've even got a women's-only cemetery. It makes sense. There must be plenty of women who've spent their lives lying under men and don't want to be buried next to them.

Kathy Lette

Sweet Mother, I can't weave my web
overcome with longing for a boy
because of slender Aphrodite.

Sappho

Tops need to be more aggressive about asking for what we want and stop acting like a bunch of victimized codependents held hostage by rapacious bottoms.

Pat Califia

Today's top
is tomorrow's bottom.

Edmund White

You know what these *arrangements* are like. You both agree you can fuck whoever you like – you're together, but totally free. In reality, it never works, someone does more fucking than the other and it ends in tears every time. But what else can you do if you don't believe in monogamy?

Hanif Kureishi

There are some who want to get married and others who don't.

Greta Garbo

Marriage is a long, dull meal
with dessert served at the beginning.

Oscar Wilde

From now on, love it or hate it,
same-sex marriage is the main event.

Gabriel Rotello

Sex is a less documented way
in which we experience culture.

Christos Tsiolkas

One's real life is often
the life that one does not lead.

Oscar Wilde

Let's face it, deep down we're all Baby Jane Hudsons, Miss Havershams and Esta Blodgetts. If we can't be allowed to see life through the rose-coloured glasses of our own invention, we'll settle for seeing it through the bottom of the nearest bottle.

Neal Drinnan

Love him and let him love you.
Do you really think anything else
under Heaven really matters?

James Baldwin

I adore to dance with them and take them to theatres and private views and talk about dresses and plays and women, but I'm really much more fond of men.

Cecil Beaton

A woman who loves a woman
is forever young.

Anne Sexton

You're neither unnatural, nor abominable, nor mad; you're as much a part of what people call nature as anyone else; only you're unexplained as yet – you've not got your niche in creation.

Radclyffe Hall

With so much hate in the world,
I'm not really interested in people
who say love is wrong.

Anne Heche

In my days I was a Pioneer
and a Menace …
Then one had to lure them to
the Breast, and now you have to
smack them, back and front,
to wean them at all.

Djuna Barnes

Being a sex radical means
being defiant as well as deviant.

Pat Califia

Sex radicals look into the heart
of sexual issues and see where
hypocrisy and oppression lie.

Kimberly O'Sullivan

Dip me in chocolate and throw me to the lesbians.

T-shirt slogan

Gay relationships don't have the same support or structures around them to enforce them to be a certain way, as heterosexual relationships do, so we make up our own stuff.

Nick Toonan

Love, and do what you like.

St Augustine

No one has imagined us.
We want to live like trees.

Adrienne Rich

We do the movies and sex clubs …
We ring late at night. We cry and we
rage. Sometimes at each other.
We laugh and eat and laugh again.
We shut down and open up.
We walk a bit in each other's shoes.
Other times we say we wouldn't be
seen dead in those shoes.

Michael Hurley

Since neither gods nor
godlike verse can move,
Break out, ye smothered fires,
and kindle smothered love.
Exert your utmost power,
my lingering charms;
And force my Daphnis to
my longing arms.

Virgil

Who touches the body, however
fleetingly, also touches the soul.

David Leavitt

Everyone is born naked
and after that, everything is drag.

Ru Paul

I was once asked whether my first
sexual encounter was homosexual
or heterosexual. I don't know.
I was too polite to ask.

Gore Vidal

Two of the happiest married
people I know, whose names I must
conceal for reasons of discretion,
are both homosexual.

Vita Sackville-West

When the fuck did heterosexuals
get the patent on home and love
and hearth and family?

Harvey Fierstein

My heart was more disgraceful,
more alone
And more courageous
than the world has known.
O passer-by my heart was
like your own.

Violet Trefusis

Courage is the price
that life exacts for granting peace.

Amelia Earhart

The rump is the secret femininity
of males, their passivity.

Jean-Paul Sartre

To tell the truth, I think every man should be fucked up the arse as a prelude to fucking women, so he'll know what it's like to be the receiver.

Germaine Greer

Labels are for filing, labels are for clothing, labels are not for people.

Martina Navratilova

What is most beautiful in virile men
is something feminine;
what is beautiful in feminine women
is something masculine.

Susan Sontag

Whenever I behold someone who possesses any talent or displays any dexterity of mind, who can do or say something more appropriately than the rest of the world, I am compelled to fall in love with him.

Michelangelo

I'm an alcoholic. I'm a drug addict.
I'm a homosexual. I'm a genius.
Of course I could be all four of these
dubious things and still be a saint.

Truman Capote

Will it come like a change
in the weather?
Will its greeting be courteous or rough?
Will it alter my life altogether?
O tell me the truth about love.

W H Auden

You can't teach what you don't know.

Wayne King

She's not here, and I'd
rather see her lovely
step, her sparkling glance
and her face than gaze on
all the troops in Lydia
in their chariots and
glittering armour.

Sappho

Sisters in love,
a love allowed to climb
Ev'n on this earth,
above the reach of time.

William Wordsworth

When you see two women
walking hand in hand,
Just look 'em over
and try to understand ...

Bessie Smith

If a bullet should enter my brain,
let that bullet destroy every closet door.

Harvey Milk

One of the many purposes of
being queer is to outrage parents.

Bruno Bouchet

Simple pleasures
are the last refuge
of the complex.

Oscar Wilde

Men fire our persons for the night,
Keep us awake, and kiss and teaze,
But ah! how different the delight
I have in cuddling dear Elise.

Anonymous

Hey, here we are
a faggot & a dyke, Black
we make good music
& write good poems
We Be – Something Else.

Pat Parker

It is better to be hated for what one is
than loved for what one is not.

André Gide

Two men can defy the world.

E M Forster

Things don't change
but by and by
our wishes change.

Proust

What careless distinctions we make.
There are pathological, unloving ways
to be straight, just as there are healthy,
loving ways to be gay. Sexuality is never
the primary determinant in someone's
capacity to care.

Stephanie Dowrick

I wore makeup at a time when even on a woman eye-shadow was sinful … From that moment on, my friends were anyone who could put up with the disgrace.

Quentin Crisp

Wherever the bird with no feet flew
she found trees with no limbs.

Audre Lorde

A minority is only thought of
as a minority when it constitutes
some kind of threat to the majority,
real or imaginary.
And no threat is ever *quite* imaginary.

Christopher Isherwood

You will never succumb to the charms of any of your sex – what an arid garden the world must be for you!

Virginia Woolf to sister Vanessa

I am tired, Beloved,
of chafing my heart against
The want of you ...

Amy Lowell

Never say I don't love you, if I have to travel across Europe sitting bolt upright, to England which I detest, braving the fury of my mother, merely to catch a glimpse of you.

Violet Trefusis to Vita Sackville-West

The course of a river is always
disapproved of by its source.

Jean Cocteau

And remember, be nice to straights.
It takes two of them to make
one of you.

Boy George

I'd've fucked anything,
taken anything ... and I did.
I'd take it, suck it, lick it, smoke it,
shoot it, drop it, fall in love with it.

Janis Joplin

The only unnatural sex act is that
which you cannot perform.

Dr Alfred Kinsey

I wonder why it is so much easier
for me to love my own sex
passionately rather than yours?

Dame Ethel Smyth

To judge from French novels;
it's always a case of copulation
or nothing; to judge from English
novels; it's always a case of nothing.
And then, the moralists – but they,
poor dears, can hardly be expected
to throw much light on such a subject.

Lytton Strachey

Why should it be a crime to love someone? No one is being forced into anything ... At sixteen you are a man and you know what you are doing. I knew what it was I was doing at sixteen. I think most people do.

Jimmy Somerville

His mysterious delicacies had
seduced me. I forgot all my human
duties just so I could follow him.

Rimbaud

Sex is not a pretty act – always sweet, tender, comfortable or understandable. We are all animals, very basic and raw.

Della Grace

Saying 'ban homosexuality'
is as ludicrous and unnatural as
saying 'ban butterflies';
the result would be just as dull.

Sarah Walker

Tell me why you play with me,
Take my heart so prettily
In your dainty, slender hands,
Bruise its tender, loving, bands?

Virginia Woolf

Where has she come from,
this moment of light?

Stephanie Dowrick

Beauty is beauty only
while you gaze on it,
but one who's good will soon
be beautiful as well.

Sappho

There's nothing I need from anyone
except love and respect, and anyone
who can't give me those two things
has no place in my life.

Harvey Fierstein

Infinite sad mischief has resulted
from the profane bursting open
of secret recesses.

Herman Melville

If I'm absolutely frank, I prefer women to men but if I'm brutally frank I'd admit I prefer chocolate to either.

Anonymous

All I know is this: If you and Papa are
responsible for the way I am, then
I thank you with all my heart, for it is
the light and joy of my life.

Armistead Maupin

The only thing I regret about my past is the length of it. If I had to live over again, I'd make the same mistakes, only sooner.

Tallulah Bankhead

So much memory,
so few rememberers.

Edmund White

We were two suns, exchanging atmospheres, drawn into each other, spiralling into one another.

Timothy Conigrave

When lovers reveal themselves to
each other ... there's something
archaic and remembered.
Some halcyon spiritual recall.

Neal Drinnan

Last night I spent in her arms –
and to-night I hate her –
which, being interpreted,
means that I adore her.

Katherine Mansfield

She came easy …
It is a very great pleasure altogether
Softly in a hotel, softly and in a hotel
softly in a hotel softly in a hotel.

Gertrude Stein

When you came, you were like
red wine and honey,
And the taste of you burnt my mouth
with its sweetness.

Amy Lowell

If it be a sin
to love a lovely lad,
On then sin I …

Richard Barnfield

Oh how I doted!

Cecil Beaton

Try a boy for a change.
You're a rich man.
You can afford the luxuries of life.

Joe Orton

There are only two times in this world when I am happy and selfless and pure. One is when I jack off on paper, and the other is when I empty all the fretfulness of my desire onto a male body.

Tennessee Williams

Mathew fucked Mark fucked
Luke fucked John
who lay on the bed that I lie on,
touch fingers as you sing this song.

Derek Jarman

I'm not willing
to just be tolerated.
That wounds my love
of love and liberty.

Jean Cocteau

What is sauce for the goose may be
sauce for the gander, but is not
necessarily sauce for the chicken,
the duck, the turkey or the guinea hen.

Alice B Toklas

There's nothing cozier or safer
than a nice little lez-nest.

Truman Capote

Any man who gets up in the morning
and tells the mirror 'You're adorable'
deserves to come to a bad end.

Clive Barker

Better blatant than latent.

early activist slogan

O Manhattan, your frequent
and swift flash of eyes
offering me love,
Offering responses to my own —
these repay me,
Lovers, continual lovers,
only repay me.

Walt Whitman

Throughout this attempt at
a relationship you've shown a greater
level of commitment to watching
'Melrose Place' than you've ever
shown towards me.

Graeme Aitken

Having sex and representing it
on film is not a turn-on. It's work.

Bruce Labruce

I may love Judy Garland, but ultimately what makes me a gay man is that I want a big one down my hunger chute.

Marcus O'Donnell

No position is impossible
when you're young and healthy.

Joe Orton

Remember ...
you're only as old as you look.

Bob Downe

In Amsterdam, everything you could want to do is right there, it gets boring. Jimmy (Somerville) and I said thank god for a bit of (English) oppression.

Andy Bell

It is an American habit to turn
complex moral problems into
technical legal ones.

Andrew Solomon

Just because I like to suck cock
doesn't make me any less
American than Jesse Helms.

Allen Ginsberg

I say if it's love
the Lord won't mind.

Gordon Merrick

I could not make love to boys
without loving them.

Jean Genet

Rubber is the ubiquitous interceptor
between fantasy and reality.

Tony Ayres

When you take a stand for anything,
you risk it. I wouldn't change a thing.

Ellen DeGeneres

memories nestled next to hearts
cardiac taboos beating beating softly

m d west

Once thou didst seek the
solace of thy kind,
The madness of a kiss was more to thee
Than Heaven or Hell, the
greatness of thy mind
Could not conceive more potent ecstasy!

Radclyffe Hall

There is one woman whom fate
has destined for each of us.
If we miss her we are saved.

Anonymous

If you wish to see someone at their worst, observe them coming in or out of a relationship.

Kerry Bashford

Love is the extra effort that we
make in our dealings with those
whom we do not like.

Quentin Crisp

That little piece of your heart that you
try to keep away from anyone –
I don't think anyone likes that exposed.

Sue-Ann Post

Human beings are too important to be
rated as mere symptoms of the past.

Lytton Strachey

Conception's just a shot in the dark.

David Wojnarowicz

Homosexuality is God's way
of insuring that the truly gifted
aren't burdened with children.

Sam Austin

Keep love in your heart.
A life without it
is like a sunless garden
where the flowers are dead.

Oscar Wilde

You'd struck history
at an angle, exposing the fault lines;
always leaning, because the world
was tilted. Pleasure came late.

Michel Foucault

Those who restrain Desire,
do so because theirs is weak enough
to be restrained.

William Blake

Strange how potent
cheap music is.

Noël Coward

Women are like banks, boy,
breaking and entering is a
serious business. Give me your
word you're not vaginalatrous?

Joe Orton

Pornography, like charity,
begins at home.

Neal Drinnan

I'd surrender my life
(and divulge all my secrets)
for a chocolate ice cream cone.

Eric Michaels

GOD HATES HOMOS
but he loves tabouli

graffiti

Resolv'd to sing no songs to-day
but those of manly attachment.

Walt Whitman

S is for sweetie sweetie and sweetie
Y is for you and u is for me
and we are happy as happy can be.

Gertrude Stein

A thing of beauty
is a boy forever.

Carl Van Vechten

There's something about matters of the heart that leads to a numbness of the brain, a chilling of the intellect and an abandonment of scruples.

Kerry Bashford

I felt very close to God ...
My friends say that's because
I was always on my knees.

Armistead Maupin

I don't expect to touch the sky
with my own two hands.

Sappho

Please, you want a brunette with
a sense of humour, a doctorate and
HIV-negative status? Good luck honey.
Love is so infrequent that you
can't put conditions on it.

Paul Rudnick

Dreams have as
much influence as actions.

Stéphane Mallarmé

We have the potential to come together as emotional, sexual beings and experience emotional ecstasy as a result of this.

Claudia Pearce

The lover is a friend
inspired by God.

Plato

The day we stop resisting our instincts,
we'll have learned how to live.

Federico García Lorca